PAUL BUNYAN'S BEARSKIN

Poems by
Patricia Goedicke

PAUL BUNYAN'S BEARSKIN

PAUL BUNYAN'S BEARSKIN

Poems by
Patricia Goedicke

Milkweed Editions

PAUL BUNYAN'S BEARSKIN

Milkweed Editions
528 Hennepin Avenue, Suite 505
Minneapolis, Minnesota 55403
Books may be ordered from the above address.

ISBN 0-915943-54-9

95 94 93 92   4 3 2 1

Publication of this book is made possible by grant support from the Literature Program of the
National Endowment for the Arts, the Cowles Media / Star Tribune Foundation, the Dayton
Hudson Foundation for Dayton's and Target Stores, Ecolab Foundation, the First Bank
System Foundation, the General Mills Foundation, the I. A. O'Shaughnessy Foundation, the
Jerome Foundation, The McKnight Foundation, the Andrew W. Mellon Foundation, the
Minnesota State Arts Board through an appropriation by the Minnesota Legislature, the
Northwest Area Foundation, and by the support of generous individuals.

Library of Congress Cataloging-in-Publication Data

Goedicke, Patricia.
    Paul Bunyan's bearskin : poems / by Patricia Goedicke.
      p. cm.
    ISBN 0-915943-54-9
    I. Title.
  PS3557.032P38   1992
  811'.54—dc20   91-14944
                                                        CIP

Cover art is a bear image from the Haida tribe.

For the Rattlesnake Ladies Salon:

Beth Ferris, Connie Poten, Dee McNamer, Jocelyn Siler,
Kate Gadbow, Marnie Prange, Sharon Barrett,
and Caroline Patterson

With love and gratitude

Acknowledgments

With thanks to the editors in whose publications these
poems originally appeared.

ACM (Another Chicago Magazine): "American Exercises"

Black Warrior: "Some Nights the Mind"

Calapooya Collage: "My Brother's Anger" (winner of the 1987 Carolyn Kizer
Poetry Prize), "In These Soft Trinities," "Frontier," and "Shadow"

The Chowder Review: "Along the Street"

Colorado Review: "On This Island"

Cutbank: "*Ubi Leones*" and "The Rain Between Us"

The Denver Quarterly: "The Emperor's Nightingale"

The Gettysburg Review: "Weight Bearing" and "The Wind that
Swept Up Great Homer"

The Green Mountain Review: "Vigil"

Hubbub: "The Color of History"

The Hudson Review: "The Goldberg Variations" and "Paul Bunyan's Bearskin"

The Kenyon Review: "The Periscope of the Eye"

Kinesis: "Directions to Go On With" and "Deer Crossing, Wild Horse Island"

The Laurel Review: "Heart/Land"

The Massachusetts Review: "Letter to Jonathan From Missoula"

The Nebraska Review: "Broth" and "The Story"

The New England Review: "On Second Thought" and "The Charge"

The North American Review: "Whatever Gray Grid"

Ontario Review: "Dad's Ashes"

Poet Lore: "Without Looking"

Poetry Northwest: "The Point of Emptiness"

The Prairie Schooner: "What Was That," "Tell Me Another," "Now, This Morn-
ing, Beaming," and "Cathay" (Winners of the 1987 Strousse Award)

The Seneca Review: "Each Day the Mind Rises"

The Southern California Anthology: "The Lake Itself"

The Southern Review: "Beyond the Mountains"

The Tar River Review: "Passports" and "So Long"

Three Rivers Poetry Review: "The Dance Hall" and "Coin of the Realm"

Woman/Poet: "If There Were A Real Voice"

"Whenever She Speaks Up," from *After the Storm* (Maisonneuve Press, 1992)

Paul Bunyan's Bearskin

I THE GOLDBERG VARIATIONS

The Goldberg Variations

THE EYE

Music pure as the desert.
In the superimposed calm
Of separate but equal equations
Dry grains, immaculate, barely touch
Each other.

And the pianist sits at the keyboard,
Hovers over it with the distant
Thin vigilance of a helicopter.

Carefully the fingers press, lift
One low hill after another

Into violent upsurges, minute
Shimmering layers of hissing
Precise grit.

But mostly the land is flat.

The tribes having been gathered together
And then suppressed
For their own good, into subdivisions,

Around every oasis
Authority's level headed
Logic has taken over:

In the bleak geometry of noon
All error has been stamped out.

And who controls the water?

As the sluice gates mechanically open,
Then close

The pianist walks the line.

Along the irrigation ditches
Joy occasionally blooms,
Puffs of sweet green,

But the small headsprings of tenderness, the tears
That began everything have long since disappeared.

No sniveling among the pyramids
And no self pity, either:

The suicide note is discovered
If it ever is, fallen
Through a crack in the floor.

How many crumpled bodies
For Pharaoh to sleep in peace? Reason
Plays itself out by number,
Covers its own tracks.

Hammered to parallel horizons,
Under the stone paw of the Sphinx
Out there in the implacable
Empires of harmony

Beware the One, Single
Imperturbable Eye
That sweeps, unbroken
From sky to sky.

A GREENHOUSE

Yet in these blinding flatlands
Suddenly a new chord crashes.

Over the strict bars of the grid
First one quarter, then an eighth,

Then a run of sixteen verticals pokes up

Like pygmies down from the forest, prime
Small figures that itch
And jiggle in their sockets.

Among the twisted cataracts,
The untamed waterfalls of the mountains

There are no plains, only deep
Wet valleys, lush
Ankle and mind cloggers.

Among the crocodiles and the orchids
Each tribe keeps to itself,

But hunched, burning, a dark
Curled into himself troglodyte

The pianist hears them, their humming
Gurgles in his throat.

The heavens being what we see
Only by glimpses, in the jungle
As moist secrets mutter
Thick-leaved, in the night

Almost he begins to sing a little, to break out
In his rough voice, abrupt
Brief spears of it raised

And then lowered:

Rummaging through a rich
Greenhouse of scarlet trumpet flowers, tangled
Intricate nests of notes

Hunger breathes through his mouth
Like a sick oboe

But even as he bows down,
Crouches over the piano

Now there is no holding back.

Groaning over the keys
In full cry, out loud

He can't stop; muscling into each footprint
Like a bloodhound,
Intelligence purrs in his fingertips

Or else shouts:

For each new species,
Each planned permutation
He knows there is another

And moans into it, lapped
In subtle ecstasies of grief.

THE PERFORMING ANIMAL

For what he is after lives
Not just in the heavens, in pure shining veils
Of clear counterpoint, the logarithms
Of the spheres

But also buries itself, beating
In someone's low chest gone to earth.

In every synagogue, in every nomad tent
Thirsting for water in the barrios
The cry rumbles like a drum:

The performing animal almost howls
But will not let go the thread.

Fathers and fortresses, lay down your arms!

Whole civilizations have been flattened
By laws that must not be left undisturbed.

Control is the one Word
Over all

But the pianist bears up under it,
Struggles to keep it human.

Good son, obedient
As he is wily,
With blunt, nimble fingers
And recently opposed thumbs

Over the elegant mathematics bent
In boundless pleasure, it's his own voice
That will not be silenced ever.

In chords mounting like rain,
Great floods of it surge
Over the barricades like armies,
Oceans sweeping through the concert hall

Until everything in it is floating,
All dry lands inundated

With packing crates, old clothes, cooking pots,
Bibles, abandoned computers
Strewn everywhere, in the ragged
Triumphant minority of mess

The pianist breaks over our stunned heads
And then mops it all up,
Squeezing from his two hands

Once more the theme
That started it all:

Winding its slow way over the land

The last faint trickle of the sound
Of someone weeping, anyone: child
Or grown man.

II HEART/LAND

American Exercises

The tall yellowhaired girl jogs smoothly past our windows,
Bobbing up and down in her wheat-colored sweatshirt
As if she were moving through water, a millionaire's yacht

That thinks it can live forever: if bombs can't be controlled
Bodies can: the experts put on their pink leotards
Like oldtime revivalists they sweet talk us every morning,
Insisting it's our duty to ourselves but of course,

What else is there? My dear it's no different
For us either, however sedentary we may be,
It's clear we too are strung out

From moment to mortal moment, since we're attached to nothing
We have to invent something:
When the last giant explosion bloats
Into vast flattening waves we dream we will ride them out

Somehow or other, if all we have is ourselves
We must protect the investment:
Flexing our valuable muscles
Tenderly we embrace each other, kneading each precious pound of flesh

We consult marriage counselors and other coaches
In training camps all over the country it's incredible
What exercises us: in padded helmets riding bicycles
We spill out into the traffic, along suburban lanes

In the name of the Gross National Product and against Yamaha
Statistics flicker in our heads, feverishly we count calories
Even as we stuff cattle with more than enough corn
To feed whole villages for years, we'd throw every bit of it away

For a mess of Lo-Cal cereal, my dear I don't understand it,
That nice yellowhaired girl, you and me,
Surely we mean no harm, if all we want is each other

And a little lean meat, flesh too solid to melt
Into anything but the imperishably thin personalities
Of the only stars we lust after, lashing our flabby legs

Over the razed golden stubble of excess we keep pumping
As hard as we can to escape noticing those other, naturally slim figures,
Emaciated brown skeletons running their own race

Right along beside us, our sleek bodies bobbing over the prairies
Like steel breasts on the move, fat carcinogenic silos
Stuffed with sinister rods pulsing, critically fermenting wheat.

My Brother's Anger

And here they are again, the duffel bags of sadness,
Shouldering their way into the house like a football team.

Mute, muscular, swollen,
Straining at the seams

Their small eyes look up
Waiting for me to open them.

Friends, how can I help you?

I want to pick you up, to cradle you in my arms
But I am too heavy myself.

Can't anyone tie his own shoes?

Speak to me, Trouble,
Tell me how to move.

My brother's anger is a helmet.

My sister's voice is a cracked flute
Talking to itself under water.

What can I offer but a sieve?

Shoving yesterday in a closet
I make small talk, smile

Rush around trying to hang up coats

But all over the house there are these dull
Enormous sacks of pain.

Stumbling over other people's leftover lumber

I keep trying to embrace them,
Battering my head against weathered flanks . . .

Every day more suicides
Among the living, more hangovers

Among the dead.

I throw myself down on the floor
Right in front of them

But it's no use: these slab-sided sorrows
Have taken up permanent residence

And will not be comforted.

Broth

bacteria vat sits
all night

growing its own greenish
blue mold

yesterday's scum floating
dreams with blurred faces

where did penicillin come from

what accidents are these
we wake up to

good or bad, plastic
unsinkable scraps litter

the bleak shores of morning

day turns up the heat
thought fish   rise from the depths

begin to bubble   specks
scoot between the ears

tag ends from all over

jostle each other, lines from the
latest show tunes   Einstein's

great gourmet   cookbook
rubs up against snaps

of drowned bodies,   oil frothing
gray flotsam headless

ideas jittering everywhere

waiting for the latest
microwave   we wonder

what new invention
next

maybe we'll read a little, try to
compose the screaming

bits and pieces of swirling
flesh

or maybe we won't   we say

to ourselves, treading water
to keep our heads clear

when does the ocean turn ugly

what's the exact temperature of fission
or fusion

tadpoles in the mind's soup
wings swoop through the sky

when does the first word
hook itself to the first sentence

something for swimmers to hold onto

On This Island

Now each seashell empties itself
of its lost life.

Scattered like castoff nail clippings,
pieces of old civilizations

on the mind's exhausted beach

in the scrape of pebbles, the forgotten
Morse Code of the shore

gradually we've been forced to shuck off
all unnecessary details – o tiniest of voices,
jittery jumping beans in the night –

on this narrow ledge stiffening
among the scuttling crabs calling
how little the adult heart can hold how much

it must, as the swift, scouring
winds strip the ground clean

of every amenity, on this island
the only savages are ourselves; old friends,
countries that used to depend on us exist

nowhere, really, though newspapers certify their presence
it's dusk now, the past is a rattle of spray
and frayed telephone wires, at the end of a tired century

which of us can stand up
under a present that's too much for anyone to bear?

Once we insisted – *Nevertheless*
we're all one – but the arteries that used to lead
generously, to the ends of the earth

are choked now, no new footprints
sprint along them, only the arthritic wheeze
of lungs struggling to leap up

into the heavens, the easy deliverance
of space travel, anything to escape

the foolishness that comes next, the vague
childish nostalgia that wells up

almost to the eyeballs,
at the end of history for me

and how many others like husks,
coconuts bobbing on the ocean

but not making any connections, sparks
fizzle and go out, on large land masses

as on the smallest atoll, in the crenellated
coral reefs of the mind

whole nations crumble into the sea
and who will be left to remember?

Each individual story
repeats itself, failing always,

condemned to do nothing but listen
like a battered receiver set washed up by the waves

over and over to the tap tap tapping on the shell wall
of whose finger? Palmetto grass frond

or new inhabitant, if the nudged bundle of small
insinuating friend frightens us it's no
earthly use: already the first tiny foot's crept

into the tent; it's the future, of course,
about to take up residence,

as the latest nuclear-powered rocket shoots off
into someone else's new world

what's left for the rest of us but to disappear
into absolute emptiness, o appalling

blankness on the horizon, invisible airships,
rafts of radiant fear . . .

On Second Thought

It's a pinball machine, it's Ms. Pacman going off
        hairtrigger, zigzag
   faster than the eye can flick

up one corridor, down another
       zap, quicksilver
   tiny pogo stick jumping
     invisible as a flea
touch one foot and the next winks
     right after it,
   amphibrach, tribrach, molossus coming
         WATCH OUT!

Multiple access image
       thrust, critical mass
   prevaricator

       LIAR!
Let's go dump all our wastes
     in the next country:

with German *lieder* in the head,
       with the Yellow Pages ringing,
   with starved children stumbling up the stairs
    and into the attic weeping

Dan says just give us two more years
       Leonard says what will we do what will we do
in the mulberry bed when nobody's there but the poor,

the city sanitation truck comes wagging its red snout
       right down Main Street it gobbles up everything it can
under the All American maple trees,

in the humming buzzing brain fog
       between one impulse and the next jiggling
  at every touch, whoosh!

each hairsbreadth of an idea bangs off
       the next one, coming around the corner
  the pattern refuses to stay still

anything like long enough to attend to it,
       the unlocatable Will
  over the radar screen of the mind jittering
    with thousands of crazed neurons crackling

so furiously of course Ms. Pacman wants *out,*
       she's eating herself up with angst,
    in the glittering Global Village

even though she says Gee Whiz kids isn't this Great,
      we can repeat any television program we want to
  at the drop of a single token

so what if the transistor chips misfire
      at least we've got something to blame,
  in the empty spaces between heads

and no bodies but size 5 13 15 etc.,
      though the arms and legs of dear words
   vanish out the window like flowerpots

somehow we keep talking to each other
    right after 60 Minutes
  with Eleanor Roosevelt and Qaddafi

with Superman and Derrida and Einstein
       and Bruce Springsteen and the President of Coca Cola
and Ronald Reagan and Dr. Strangelove on a white horse

at the end of the Arcade something electrical's leaking,
   sparking and spitting from the fuse box but what is it?
  In the middle of the shopping mall on Saturday

with kids from high school, with the cake sale,
   with a few Vietnamese smelling of old clothes,
  with more and more South American leftists
   and a lost Philippine schoolteacher born every second

it won't stay still, it keeps moving and moving,
   it should be easy to say what's short-circuiting the System
  is thermonuclear, the threat of the Red Telephone ringing
    but it's not.

Coin of the Realm

So what if the underside of it's
not silver

no lining but cheap

nickels dimes quarters
in a change purse, the

flip side

of the coin we need to
protect ourselves, whatever

income tax we pay
for guns helps keep us in

schoolbooks

he said, tucking away the
popular rifle under the car seat

outside the playground

for emergency use
only

wouldn't you agree

in order to make an omelet
you have to break some

for most experiments to succeed

the price of conquering disease
comes high

heads, tails

after the carnage the crack
dealers return like jackals

sniffing

the shells of several hundred
Chevrolets litter the beach

then there are the claws

my father the defense contractor
in order to put bacon on the table

one hand snaps at the other
in slippery pockets the
raw jingle of scratch

sometimes bleeds a little

unfortunately, he said
stepping all over his children's

lives and not even
noticing

first it's the left side of the brain
then it's the right

in the clockwise and counterclockwise
whirl of water

into a drinking glass, the clasp
and unclasp of atoms

the terrified heart listens
for the other half of its beat

he said, realistically
speaking

it is a sad fact

in a missile silo near Great Falls
Montana

it takes two men to count

without both of them nothing
would go off

Beyond the Mountains

Until we feel it ourselves

In our own stomachs, ribs
Squashed in, dented

Pain has no shape

In concentration camps
And hospitals, on the back wards

On the page of photographs might even be a laugh
Until the label goes on

Pain has no face

Comes and goes with the wind
Which makes no sound

Of itself, only passes
Over an invisible bottle

With no mouth, no lips
Until we put them there

Who hears anyone's thoughts
At midnight

Because we refuse to look

Across the street, an old woman
Holds emptiness in her arms

Each prisoner's cell's flooded

Until we unlock it, enter
Breathe the same water

To listen is to live

On the raw edge of bodies,
Hard objects vibrating

Even when we make love

Wrapping ourselves in tight strings
Wound, then unwound

Pain makes no sound

Of itself, only turns
And turns like a sick dog

In the dirty barrios, the ghettos
Just across the street

The air's full of shouts

Crackling across shortwaves
High frequencies whine

Beyond tropical mountains
No one dares climb.

Weight Bearing

Opening the door to a fat person
Is like drowning, sometimes you think you can't stand it,

What are all those immense, painfully thick slabs

Of skin built up to hold out
Or in?

Poured into himself like concrete,
Like a candle big as an elephant that has gone out,

Sweat beads on the forehead
Of the young Kiowa sitting in my office.

With hair so black you'd think it came from a box,
In shirts fragrant with Tide,

With sides drooping all over my tiny chair
Like a grand piano in soft sculpture

He lets kids climb on him like puppies.

The murmur of his soft voice
Surrounds all sides of the subject like honey,

But if he is a messenger what has he got to say?

Wind passes its rough hand over the keyboard,
Then sighs.

In the vast folds of his body

First there is the hissing of warm breath,
Then there is all that flesh pressing against its own belt buckle.

How does he manage to sit, stand, breathe?
But he does, he tells me he's not had a drop to drink for months

And I believe him: self pity in liquid form
Is poison he doesn't need.

Besides, he has his own pupils to think of.

Back home on the reservation
The river is beginning to dry up.

The old stories disappear: whose grandmother
First spoke with Harvest Woman,

Whose uncle thought he could trick Coyote . . .

Next door a gang of white sociologists discusses the matter loudly,
Quarreling like magpies.

But who has time nowadays to listen?

The traffic ticket for speeding, the pain
Visiting his parents in a Home,

These things sink into the ground like blood,
Like antelope oil into earth

That has absorbed too much.

Expanding into the room like a balloon
Hotter and hotter, it is about to burst

And the young man knows it, he tries to say something,
Anything, at the center of himself he is starving,

He thinks he is a wild leaf snapping against the sky
And then folding, when there is no breeze

What food should he take to soothe him?

Heavy with lard, with the children heaped up on his back
He bows to suffering like a gentleman.

Out there on the mesa he is a lone cottonwood
Muttering to itself in the wind.

Anxious as a smoke signal looking left right left right
Finally there is no comforting the dry purplish lips

That shape words out of the air like waterless clouds
Scouring the land for sustenance.

Along the Street

(IN SAN MIGUEL DE ALLENDE)

The first time we noticed them, the dried up splotches of blood,
    Little maroon buttonholes trailing along the street,

Cautiously we began following them, on either side of the dark drops
    Twisting between the feet of the busy, oblivious citizens.

And though there was no one in sight, no freshly bleeding victim,
    Somehow it all seemed so ordinary, even familiar,

Though the nightstick pulse in our heads kept hammering,
    Later we barely remembered hearing it,
        The quickly snuffed-out moan

Of the cracked, goatfoot man stumbling on his heels
    Like a clumsy puppet, nailed to the crossarms of his guards
        Who kept playing with him, jerking him along like a bone.

As the size of the drops increased, approaching the police station,
    Right in front of the Supermarket there was a huge puddle of it,
        Reflecting the shiny rows of clothes, automobiles, tin cans,

In Seoul or Latin America, Russia or the United States,
    It doesn't matter which, the labels are interchangeable

And the prisoner too, usually it's someone who doesn't like stores,
    Hates armies, spies on invoices, prefers art to advertising,

But surely no one to get excited about,
    We keep telling ourselves, violence is only natural, it dries up
        As soon as it hits the streets,

So what are we doing here, in real life
    Men beating up on each other make no noise
        Unless you're right behind them,
            The thud of the punches is muffled,

But by then we were at the police station, next to the Supermarket,
 And we breathed a sigh of relief,
  For the victim, of course, had vanished
   As he always does, on the frightened trail of our lives,

So we went right back to business, we walked into the store's mouth
 Like plankton into a whale's gullet,

We tried not to notice them, the cash registers with their shark's teeth
 Ominously ringing, clanking their steel gears,

We kept a tight lid on it, in the stockroom behind scenes
 We kept looking nervously over our shoulders,

We knew it would be too much like opening a can of sardines
 Or a bottle of catsup, you have to be very careful

Not to spill anything, to be a good citizen
 You have to keep your lips sealed, you mustn't stop for anything,
  But just keep on walking, walking along the street.

Heart/Land

And now the little bundles of ache hang inside
Like pronged blood berries on their branches. Hooked

Blisters coat the underside of veins

As children's jackets pile up in the cloakroom
Where it's dark, where nobody comes all day.

So the deposits clutter and grab onto each other.

Fat feeds on itself in packed
Hard bubbles growing inward

Until I am near choked with it,
What can I hear, what can I see out of such small eyes?

Earlier it seemed somehow more bearable.

Even when they turned sour, when life turned poison
Those black buckets were meant to be discussed.

When fear came, when the ceiling filled with bats,
All we had to do was talk about them and they'd go away,

And in that democracy I had high hopes.

Pain was a minority I wore on my sleeve
And others wore it too,

But comforting each victim
Efficiently, each starving child like experts

Naturally we had to comfort ourselves first:
How else could we have managed?

In order to be able to help them

We had to keep our own families fed.

But that only smoothed the way for the silent
Clogged channels of the pileup,

For the twigs soon broke, of course,
Without my knowing it, how

When I was so well adjusted, able
To explain away even great grief

Where did the bodies come from?

Almost overnight
Exercise is never enough, nor charity

Nor any amount of preparation.

Now, squeezed in here by my own greedy
Occupying armies

After all those years of belief,
Saying the same thing over and over,

– The President is coming, the President is coming –

It seems we have rushed to the seaside only
To cast away our votes.

For the bottles are coming back now,
The messages we sent unread,

But what could any of us have done
I ask you, muffled up to the gills

In brown bags, grapes from every world,
Each feeling or idea

Or person we had to put aside

Because there was no time, there is never any time,
In the precincts of deferred pain

Crushed in here under all these thick carpet rolls

Of course there are no ballots, there are never any ballots
For those who will not speak.

On this aging continent,

In the padded interior of an end
I refuse to believe in,

We are crowded out, gasping for air

And losing it to our sick hearts:
In swollen antechambers pinned

Globes of denied suffering cluster
Just beneath the skin.

Ubi Leones

They are where they always are. Prowling.
Behind shuddering baseboards low growls,
Waves of them, the soft pad of feet
Stalking the borders that stand between us
And all that is not us. But we watch;
We will not let them in.

                    We keep lying to ourselves,
"No, there's nothing important out there,"
The gust of song that blurts from an open window
And then stops, suddenly, stumbling over our quarrels,
Cruel words, insults, that time I made you weep

                    No, I will not pursue it!
That would be to be swept right off the charts
On all fours, in bleak deserts howling
And rolling my head, with wide open jaws
Terrified by the shapes of all I have done
And not done.

                    Rather than face them down
In their own kingdom, let us go out and buy barbed wire,
Bombs, helicopters, Kalashnikovs;
Anything to keep the barbarians at bay,
As long as they keep sending us kisses
And cheap clothing, as long as they keep us warm, vital, "in touch"

                    At a safe distance from the drums throbbing
Out there at the edge of the world, if it's not rage
Rising up against us, knives in the hands of children,
It's the obscenity of a finger: whatever we try to put down
Mushrooms itself overnight

                    Because they are still there, the lions,
Those monarchs we have loved secretly, always,
In cramped zoos they pace behind dingy bars

By day only; on long nights they roam the windy savannahs
Restless as cars, in the streets we hear them calling,
For we may not escape them, in the darkening mind's disorder
There are no frontiers to pain,

                              Even the toughest membrane
Cannot hold out against it; in quiet living rooms behind curtains
The sarcasm mounts, in the rubble of ruined cities
Like snipers from broken windows, with snarls not just for our enemies
But whatever interferes with us, suddenly
The tongue slips, or the trigger finger

                 And there they are, in a great cloud,
A gold floating of manes
Over the tall superhighways and the tollbooths
Secretly the shadow passes, so high in the sky
The ache of it cannot be stopped, in the red champ of rage

                       The forms we see are our own;
From grim treetops, sleek muscular shapes leaping
That cannot be turned back, as the houses of our lives fall down
Pain is the only password; as the maps disappear,
As the colors of all countries fade
And bleed across rivers, in the jungle that surrounds us all

                    They are launching themselves already
In broad daylight, hurling themselves down
On someone we know, on the paralyzed piece of flesh looking up
From the ground below us, at the end of the bloody race
The last thing most of us see will be the white sun
Exploding beneath us, the agonized dazzle of terror frozen
On a friend's face.

III VIGIL

The Charge

The father's hands are beautiful
but grasping, they reach up out of the rented bed
like crabs in a bucket, the scrolled
blue ropes of the veins stand out like pincers
that will not let go, it's dangerous to come near them
and the sons know it, where is the mother?

In the chill room they lean down over the bars of the bed
as if it were a crib, as if to one of their own children
and the father's hands clamp down, they lock onto their wrists
with the steely grip of babies but worse, much worse,
what can a father hold onto
if not his sons? The mother is beyond caring,
in the distance there are fires. A window turns into a door
that won't open, though he begs them to open it they can't,

no one can. The trees stand around like jailers
with their backs turned, rustling against the streaked sides
of the old farmhouse. Moths fly against bleak
bars of light, rectangles flattened out over dark grass
into the night. Beyond the spotlight, out there
the audience vanishes. In here like a boxer
clutching at the ropes, the struggle dwindles down
to a single figure, exhausted, sprawled on the bare ground.

Except for the sons, if there are any.
Over the strange crib they lean in
to the gaunt ribs arched up to them on the bed.
Green medicine drools from the mouth
and they wipe it off, someone with a soft cloth
soothes the glistening forehead. While the sons watch
helpless, staring at the harsh planes of the cheeks

days have gone by, it seems years
since the father first chained them to his side.
Still, one of them lifts the old man's clenched fist

to his own lips and holds it there
hour after hour, brooding. Dressed in his smart T-shirt,
his wristwatch that tells time to the microsecond,
he pores over his father's face
with the profound absorption of a lover.

Are there tears salted behind the son's eyelashes?
He shakes his head, no. The hay bailer rattles around the field
in a fume of diesel and beer. The father cannot hear it
but the sons can, they think of their own sons at home,
they plan the rambles they will take
when they return, speaking to them of their grandfather,
holding their hands like soft pieces of cotton,
five pudgy fingerlings that used to cling
like monkeys, to their father's fat thumbs

and then grew up, grew stronger,
the fathers are desperate to be with them
right now, imagining them calling their names – Dad? –
from the last pocket of emptiness before sleep retrieving them
for a few hours, over the sickroom they hover
like a fling of sparrows, in their fathers' heads braided
this once into one many-fibered strand

that will last the night. And though it will surely break
one day, for now it is an iron charge like a bar
that flows from the top of the oak straight through the sons' shoulders
and into the father's body like rage. For the sons will not let go,
they will hold on till the end. Slabbed, implacable, somber,
slow moving as rocks that will only be moved
when they want to be, there is a silence here
of stone monuments: as if grief had any say in the matter,
as if love had any power.

Vigil

Round green face on the table, clock dial
      flowering

and radio. Indistinguishable crackle
      of voices

all night next to the echoing cave
      of the old man's cold
            ruthless skull.

Littered around him the daily
      soiled artifacts: Neo-Sinephrine,
            throat lozenges,

air purifier, brown plastic slippers,
      rumpled underwear thrown
            in a bleak corner:

far above, out of sight
      the vast glittering palms
            of the Milky Way turn.

Nearer there are hair ribbons,
      tiny lights in the houses.

The metal suitcases of war
      drag past windows

he won't look out of, not for
      any need but his own,

so his children think,
      who know nothing,

but cast away the godhead
      and the prince
            into darkness falls

and there lies. Who sees
        none but himself
                sees nothing

or everything: what price warmth
        in an empty bed?

Blind sleet rasps
        over bent snow fences:

salt cellars turned over
        and running out

as whole civilizations
        vanish

into an old man's one
                lone outpost:

all night the vigil,
        the pure stubbornness of it,

the quiet radio that purrs
        sometimes mysteriously, sometimes
                just talks to him, says

less and less as the clock ticks,
        nerves twitch,
                almost gutter out.

As no children call, or wife,
        in the darkness a box of pills

gleams dully, illuminated
        by neon light.

Dad's Ashes

Someone forgot where they were,
with Mom long gone, imagine
Dad's ashes, for how many years,
on which lopsided shelf
of the garage, which exact, greasy
cardboard container,
how many old mattresses
did he look down on,
what dead paint buckets
in wadded corners what crumpled
stale newspapers announcing which fat
rich nation recently invaded which poor one?

In the kitchen occasionally we'd wonder about them
and then forget again, drinking coffee.
As each year went by
quick as a window, a box car
on a jerky train that stopped once
just for a second, with a jolt
in the garage's dark siding,
none of us ever left home
not really, not for good,
maybe because we kept hearing them
every so often, those noises
of shadows moving, rustles
behind bicycle wheels whispers
and brief flashes, shrill
needles of sound high up
near the collarbone

and then ignoring them:
John, for instance,
was laughing in the garage
the day after he got married, untying
the telltale white
ribbons from the rear bumper

why should he have remembered?
And Jenny wept out there, bawling
like a small cow because she couldn't
raise any money for the slum kids
plus, her own friends jeered at her
for a bleeding heart.

The day John first noticed the odd
lump under his arm he was straining
to jack the car up: later
as the cancer slowly ate
everything out from under
the hood of his chest,

he came to the garage to curse,
kick at tires
or, in the bathroom, after his wife
finally left him, *Dad,*
he might have thought,
*what did you do with yourself
after Mom died?* hands
stopped cold, in soapy water, in the clean
run-down house with no
escape from it,

in broad daylight, in blue
exhaust fumes, an engine's rattling snarl
of course he'd hear them, sometimes
hovering overhead
hushed, in a kind of pale
heavy column, a clotted
transparent vague sense
of *something there*

though it was soft Jenny
who found them at last, on the top
shelf next to the cracked
storm window, and swore

and then sighed,
and carefully took the grimed
anonymous box out
to the clear creek, planted
her high heels in mud, then sowed
the moving waters with Dad's sandy
gray flakes
like pieces of oatmeal,
dry bread crumbs for birds
to follow with their beaks, drifting
on calm currents to the sea

wouldn't it be nice to think? John says
as he and Jenny board
a superjet to the next
last chance clinic, high over
the rustling creek the plane
stitches the sky like a tiny
fierce needle sharpening itself
smaller and smaller until the precise
minute point of it sinks
out of sight, suddenly
into air

Without Looking

Either at my friend's daughter's
sixteen year old body dumped
on the morgue slab, T-shirt
stuck fast to one ripped
breast I identified
quick, and then
got out of there

or at the old gentleman
with tubes in the living room, spittle
stained in his wispy
beard, out of
the corner of my eye I hardly
notice it, how

could I, drink in hand
at five-thirty, at the least
sign of pain one of us always itches
to turn away, another turns
over in sleep, groans
O, we who are so lucky

just to be able to
ignore, go back
quick, to our books, to
have books, even, how
difficult it is to look
hard and head
on has not been said

often enough, if prayer
is an act of attention
even to dropped stitches, blood
dangling beneath the lines, the
poem? I said,
*what prepares us for what
will never save us?*

The Emperor's Nightingale

Grizzled face over the formica
next to the mirrored toaster.

In the glare of Venetian blinds
and your faded bathrobe, the plaid

burning flash of an eye.

The bland refrigerator whirrs
and goes off.

"Hans Christian Andersen", we were just saying
when the emperor's gold nightingale clanks into the room,

perches itself on the windowsill and begins singing
its little song.

And hearing it, suddenly
dabbing tissues at our cheeks

we find ourselves weeping

the bitter tears of Art
without Life, that Art reminds us of.

****

Nor is this the cruelest.

In Auschwitz, at the command
of a dying she-Nazi

a woman with shaved head and lice

over the dead bodies
of all her relatives must sing

Madame Butterfly's lament.

The enchanted sweetness breaks
out of scabbed lips

once more for both women:

uniformed bosom gags, sobs
as broken hearted

as anyone.

****

For the corpses pile up everywhere:
in the middle of everyone's kitchen

grief cannot be contained but starts up,
as the cry streaks across the air

Art's immortal metal
soars out of reach and stays there.

And here in the chill morning

with you nearing the end,
myself fast approaching,

we who would hold each other always
can only listen

as the old story repeats itself: this once in the world
then never

the philodendron's green
leaps at the blinds like an animal.

****

So, when I thought to sing
over the telephone, for my father

wracked on his deathbed

once more the chorus
of the song he wrote for my mother,

husky, into the black mouthpiece
my voice stuttered and broke,

I tried to finish it
and could not:

the key stuck in my throat.

IV THE RAIN BETWEEN US

Whenever She Speaks Up

Frieda, one of Gulliver's little-known Brobdignagian mistresses,
wakes up to find herself tied down, trussed to the pavement like some big
beautiful dirigible in the middle of a crowded intersection
just outside Washington, D.C.

Gulliver, why have you forsaken her? Cars drive
their black tires over her thighs.
Democracy indeed! And the nights are worse.
Cockroaches, half finished ideas
climb all over her body.

Meanwhile, in the Halls of Justice,
one or two ex-fighter pilots and a few nervously
dithering basketball players are sending her kids off to war.
What if she grabbed up a handful of gunboats
and waded the glorious Potomac after them?

Whenever she speaks up, instantly
they rape her down.
Some of them just want to crawl back where they came from
with gun and camera, occupy her womb.
How can she help but bleed over them, massive rivers of arrogant
fraternity brothers murdering other people's children?

Crazed legislators like mosquitoes, midget cars run amok
scourge all but the money makers from the Rotunda.
In the stale, black rubber smell of overload
sweat stands up on her neck like tumors, her brain refuses to lie down.

Short-circuited, she keeps waiting for thunderbolts, some long ago lost
electrical connection. What could the Author have been thinking of,
turning so many of his offspring against each other?
She wonders why she ever paid any attention to Him in the first place:
Him with his little stick.

Now, remembering the nursery, the video games and the toy golf clubs,

the 28 flavors of ice cream she fed him whenever he asked,
Frieda picks up Gulliver from the sidewalk, she pinches him with her thumb.
She can't *stand* him; she says she would rather suffocate
in her own vomit than have anything more to do with him.
But he is her son.

If There Were A Real Voice

After the TV's turned off, the last kiss
The current magazine thrown down next to the bed

Who is that old crone hunched in on herself, mumbling
And rocking in my head?

Bits of trash drift
In the darkness between my eyes.

In clusters of half finished ideas

Each picture I have made of the world bleeds
Into grainy newsprint, shredded pieces of paper

In limp curls settling on the floor of the mind
And then starting up again, hovering

As if they had something to say but no
Nothing, with the pillow pressed against my cheek

I keep trying to catch up with them but they won't stay long,

In quick scurries, rumpled
As the old woman's laddered stockings

They scratch like passing dog thistle and are gone.

And nothing I can do will stop them.

Occasionally the fluid gallop of a deer
Flares across the field, the violent flower of a volcano

Or your snore lights up the sky:
Someone outside, proof of something beyond?

But after all who are you
Sleeping beside me in your body

After sixteen years still no real answer.

By day it seems easy: sentence follows sentence
In brief lockstep around the house

Things do as they're bid: letters arrive on time
With votes taken, budgets, smiles over the daffodils

But something's missing, the minute the light's turned off

What was it I wanted to remember, a line of poetry
On the six o'clock news, you saying *I love you*

But can't help you, small animals skitter behind the woodwork
In bits and pieces, never the one great cat

We long for, slouched out there in the mountains

How can anyone help anyone

If this is all we have what is my real name
How can anyone stop searching

Everywhere, under the bitter garbage of stars
All I want is one clear thought that will stay

If not here in the haphazard,
The grizzled interior flickering

Where is it, in the back alleys of the head like snow
At the end of evening, over all the television sets hissing

If there were a real voice what would it say
And whose would it be, let it not be my own

Or let it: in my fifty-ninth year I'm still looking for it
Each night my address changes, where is my real home?

In These Soft Trinities

Whenever I see two women
        crowned, constellated friends

it is as if three birch trees wept together
        in a field by a constant spring.

            The third woman isn't there

exactly, but just behind them a flame
        bursts out, then disappears

in a blurred, electric shining
        that lifts my hair like an animal's.

In an aura of charged air I remember
        my poor mother turned into royalty,
            my sister and me in bobby socks

endlessly, all summer long
        calling each other Margaret Rose

and Lillibet, Lillibet, Lillibet,
        pretending to be princesses...

Now, swollen into these tall blooms
        like paper cutouts in water,

in each new neighborhood garden
        always, two women talking

nod their three curly heads together:
        with bits of dirt on their foreheads, speckled
            iris, flaming poppy

in the backyard dynasties of the multiflora
        it is the famous funeral photograph
            of the Dowager Queen, Queen Mother, stunned Young Queen,

three stepping stones in marble
      that haunt me forever, clear
           and mysterious as well water, the weight of it

in a bronze bucket swinging
        powerfully from my hand.

As the plumcolored shadow rises,
      full as a first child in the orchard,

the lost gardening glove on the path,
        the single earring tucked

        in an odd corner of the purse and then found

here double themselves, then triple:
      in these soft trinities
        the lives that begin in us

are born and born again like wings.
      Secret as doves scuffling

in the wide envelope of wombs
        like loose, comfortable aprons flung

over the heads of friends leaning together
      in the hum of earth's plainsong

like a three part round,
      like a single voice murmuring
        the dream never leaves us, of the self

like a three masted vessel still voyaging:
      out of the long matrix of memory,
        the royal bulbs in the hold,

the ballast that keeps us upright, loyal
        to the dark, deep-bedded throne
      of the old country each new soul claims as its own.

Tell Me Another

Each Saturday swaddled in it, the delicious
pretend boat of air,
beneath white sheets, in the queer milky light
the bedclothes lazily flap.
Drifting between sleeping and waking
these summertime mornings, luminous,
picking at scabs and scratching,
How many mosquito bites do you have?
My sister's skinny brown leg like a pretzel
pokes itself up to be inspected:
lapped in the soft fragrance of grass,
of soda pop on a hot sidewalk,
even the smell of bacon won't budge us.
So tell me a story! my sister nudges
and slowly I begin, but suddenly,
What's that?
My eyes dazzle at it:
green, leafy, enormous,
a huge rustling Face looms
hungrily, pressing its blurred features to the window
until I refocus:
back in our billowing cocoon
safer by far to concentrate
on whatever's nearest:
my sister's big toe
and then mine sticks straight up,
strides across the stage like the Colossus
both of us like to dream of but right now,
rolling over on the cool pillows,
Tell me another, my sister murmurs,
as calm as if we were lounging
on the great Nile, on Cleopatra's barge,
the silk walls of the pavilion swell outwards
and so I pick the bedpost,
in pineapple mahogany turbanned
a Nubian slave, this time –

but popping her fat tongue
psst, bong, like a tennis racquet –
Come on, let's go have breakfast, says my sister
and I wince, with all my rosy toes I know
soon enough they'll be calling us
to get up, brush our teeth this minute!
In waterless boat yards docked
in the busy packing plants of the real
like lame polliwogs, cute pigs to market
there's no stopping any of it:
already the stories we used to tell, the visions
and even the revisions fade,
in the dry slaughterhouses of duty
at the clock's alarm you wake
as I do, in a strange city,
but still, rubbing sleep from our eyes
and grumbling, clinging hard to the salty
pale outlines of a sail,
with linen threads hovering
like smoke, like mist rising from the ocean,
each morning I forget, drowsily
in these few vanishing seconds
Don't go, I say to my husband, *Please,
Not yet, not yet.*

What Was That

Whenever floor boards creak in the wind
On the old porch, unprotected
The bare planks speak only to themselves

In a voice I know,
Whenever I open my mouth I hear it,

The hollow intake of air
Just before one starts singing the hum

Of the sound that is not sound exactly
But whatever shapes it:

At the concert in Carnegie Hall
My mother, clutching her pink coat

And holding her breath in the back row,
Swore she could hear my soprano

Out of 250 others in the chorus
Soaring, loud and clear. . .

Adjusting the Sonitone in her deaf ear
– What was that? –

I still see her, cocking her head like a squirrel
Among taxicabs, movie marquees, restaurants,

Up five flights of rickety stairs she gasped
– No problem! – to my proud cold water flat.

Now, thirty-five years gone by,
Some door downstairs opens
And instantly all the dresses whisper.

I have a drawer full of lost gloves

Sonatas with one page missing

But out of the near silent closet
Of her childhood

However she used to rage at us
Those mornings, the pinched hearing aid forgotten,

In the living room, after supper
Straight up from the tingling floor

With hot faces wheeling
To the pound of Beethoven, the sweet
Barn swallow swoop of Tchaikovsky

Laughing, she'd send us leaping – *Ar-a-*
besque! – higher than any homework

And happier, even though she'd jerk away
Next morning, brusque as the thick mittens she knitted for us
With sharp bursts of cinnamon on her tongue

In winter, on the front porch
Out here in Montana how she would have stood out

In all weathers passionately listening and listening
To the wild roar of great trees

And calling after them, breathless
In her husky alto

This time it is I who can hear her
Whenever I open my mouth

In the exact same voice now
As then, whenever floor boards creak in the wind.

Now, This Morning, Beaming

Three girls on their bicycles
              at the corner of Valley Road
                        rest, lazily
        slim arms on chrome handlebars
                              Where To Next
                  doesn't concern them,
        maybe a cherry coke
                        at Putnam's

awkward as little goats
                      with scratched legs dangling
          the secret places
                              are still secret
          what the music does to them
the sudden wild *swoop*
                    right out of the body
          they never mention

but this morning, seeing
                    on Nancy's delicate pink
                              eggshell cheeks
          – oh delicate
                    as violets,
Botticelli tendrils! –
                  damp hair
                              right there on the street

one of them can't help it:
                              "Nancy," she says,
        "don't be embarrassed, but honestly
                        this morning, on your bicycle
                  you are more beautiful
          than anything I've ever seen!"

then waits, fiddling with the hand brake
                              for Nancy to laugh at her, sneer

what then but darkness
                              a dead world, stillborn
                    stopped in its tracks

while a car goes by, a wind
                    of warm tar,
          thumped tennis ball thwacked
                              on a tennis court
which Nancy does not hear
                              nor does she move
          with no hint of a tease she nods
                    thank you, a grown woman
                              already
          in cutoff jeans she acknowledges
                    the possibility

so that the other wants to jump
                    right off the edge of the sidewalk
                              through every thicket
          she'll ramp her bicycle
                    jubilant, over winter rocks

pay her own way
                    around the world
          whatever she may meet
                              she wants to shout
                    now, this morning, beaming
          it is as if she had opened her window
                              to the gorgeous sun just coming up
and been hit on the head, gently
          a great slap

Passports

"Naah," she says, voice too low for a wheedle
                              too high for a sneer
     "Geez," what do we have to learn grammar *for?*
                         in the 6th grade, in New Hampshire
               end of her first year in America
     this is what it has come to:
                                   quick as a chipmunk, leggy
               in her long American jeans
     her Maw and Paw may weep
                    over her Chinese food, out of their Chinese eyes
                    but not her, never

then what is it
     when she plays the piano
                    what is that rustle of silk
                              I keep chasing after, bamboo groves
                    under the black fence of her hair
          the beautiful birthmark on her temple
                    like a brown rose

"Geez," she says, "Sure I'll give you music lessons,"
                         she makes me sit on the grass
                              learn every note by sight, precise
                    patient as an ant
          after Juilliard she takes up geology
                              then microbiology
                    sterilizes chicken eggs
                              in a laboratory

earlier, reading Shaw together
                         then Mozart, then Freud,
     Shakespeare, Hemingway, Whitehead
                         while the rest of the team raced
                    elbows flying, breathless
     at field hockey we chose to be fullbacks, lounging
                         in deep grass near the goal

of course I was making it up
                              where she was going
              was no more mournfully romantic
                      than it was tragic
          riding our bikes to Girl Scouts
                                      in her light voice, frisky
"Heck, yes," she'd say
                          "I want to be an American"
          I would have followed her anywhere
                              but there.
It was the China Sea I was after
                  and music, and literature, and Art
          not Occum Pond, her father teaching religion
                  to the Dartmouth Indians
                          but greater waters, enormous
          smoky in her eyes

I knew she wanted to be a cheerleader
                          like everyone else and couldn't
          anymore than I could, with my thick glasses, my fat,
                  then what was it
                          the two of us aliens together
          back there when minorities
                              were still suspect

I thought what we were interested in was the mind
                              in Mexico when we traveled
                      she was more beautiful than ever
          La China Poblana
                  the Chinese citizen, they called her

but she made me take off my Girl Scout uniform for the men
                      right down to my green soul
          scared at first, then growing
                          with so many warm beds in the world
                  brown muscles, yellow
          eventually even white

what I found was my dumb Irish
contented self

what sort of passport
did she find
when she finally went back to China was she too late
or too smart
now she throws pots
in Berkeley
with two daughters and a mathematician
for a husband

this is what it has come to
after twenty years in Mexico
now I write poetry
in Montana
often her gold face
weaves quizzically across mine
in Glacier Lake
the Irishman I married
is half handsome Chinese
half Russian Jew.

Cathay

(FOR MARGARET FOX SCHMIDT)

Even after the chemotherapy I said O you
Perfect roundness of celestial fruit
I'm nuts about you.

Your cupcake face sits
In the middle of the gold star of your hair
Like a child's picture of the sun smiling

You fly over our heads such a bright snappy flag
Fuzzy with peach bloom but crisp,
Jaunty as a pirate,

What's in your hold is a mystery,
But cutting through the deep blue seas of your eyes
The tart juices spurt up, delicious

As candied ginger from Cathay
And I'd load you into my market basket
Any day: there you'd roll around

Like a pale yellow grapefruit rubbing cheeks
With lesser creatures; dull turnips, potatoes
For you're not only the cream, you're the citrus in my cargo,

Just listening to you tell stories makes me want to jump up,
Hearing about all those swashbuckling ladies,
Your heroic chuckle like the rough chunk of waves

Keeps slapping at my sides with such encouraging spanks
I just wanted to tell you, for a Kewpie doll you're some dame,
For a gun moll you're some sweet seagoing daisy;

With your round face waving to me from the bridge
If just being around you for two minutes turns me into a brandied apricot
All dippy and dizzy and brave as a gangster bee

With one arm and a broken leg
All you'd have to do is say *Vamanos!*
And I'd follow you anywhere, honey.

Many Houses

(FOR PAT GREAN)

And many paintings of houses
                           in this one
                  ordinary Ohio   split level
        the spaces around   each picture
                           on white walls   halos
                  of calm air drifting
        each in its own   place

Returning   turning off   the engine
                           still ticking
              back there in town
                           so many people   racing
                  down the basketball court
        horns blaring   electric

Slowly relaxing   I sink
                  into this orderly
              easy silence   you've made
        so many objects   rescued
                           blue willow   Chinese bowls
                                    rest

On walnut tables   or oak
                  stones in a stream   gleaming
                           with newspapers   even encyclopedias
                  in black leather   the latest
        reclining chair next to embroidered
                                    by hand   bright
                  cherry and mahogany burlap
                        throw pillows

The houses in the paintings   stare
                           as if there were nobody in them
                  only the breath of plants

                    transparent
            milky shadows
        glowing

Outside   on the deck
            bird feeders jammed
                    with olive cardinals   and scarlet
            mild chickadees flash
                        against the glass
            reflected

As cloud tracks
            over clapboards
                    voices cry out   like steel
        bicycles hold out their handlebars
                        in the scrape of snow shovels
            echoing

Here nothing   may be overlooked
            even suffering   has its place
        old friends   in the living room
                            the swift dip of hands
            gaunt cheekbones   a child's
                        remembered hair
            lifting

Red hillside of a stocking
                leafless tree   of the spine
        I see you separate
                leaning against the counter
        white sheets flap   in the sunshine
                    pale billowing fragrances
            we can't see

You who have made this   welcome
                    for so many years   set
            the front door ajar
        whether the houses are empty   or not

              doesn't matter   who knows
        in the spaces around
                              each one
    if nobody lives in them   or someone
              just about to come home

So Long

I said to my old friend, *What's
the matter, why don't you call
anymore?* But she shrugged, pretended

she hadn't heard me. Bumping
my shopping cart clumsily
right next to hers I wanted to scream

among the wet cabbages
by the broccoli's cold breath
What is it you're doing, how can you

after all those intimate
backyard get-togethers, deep
serious conversations over

the last bourbon of the night,
coffee next morning to hash
everything out, make sense, interpret

carefully, the significance
of each separate nuance
of feeling, idea, whatever

could possibly help explain
how one might live, believing
we live only on understandings

just like ours, mature, settled
at habit's comfortable board,
but here by the brand new, flash frozen

exotic fruits, sugary
red mangoes, huckleberries
in brandied syrup with nuts, humdrum

loyalty vanishes fast.
Someone I don't know taps her
on the arm just as I start planning

how to continue: *Hey look!*
I'd say, brightly, but instead
she passes right on by me, smiling

at someone else but fiddling
so nervously with her hair
I'm worried; is she all right, shouldn't

we try to talk about it?
But next to the garbage con-
tainers probably it's got nothing

to do with me, those splotches
of sudden red on her cheeks,
leathery as the dry pomegranates

of approaching age mean just that:
the fine stew of first friendship's
over, bring on the next, something's

got to be done to stop it,
some vital elixir, bubbling
new relationship to help forget

there's no avoiding the rot
waiting for all of us; at least
so I comfort myself she's thinking,

with jaws tight as old lemons,
with cold cauliflower feet
clamped to the soiled sawdust on the floor

at last I agree with her:
What's a chat with an ex-friend,

even a good one, to chase after?

If even canned goods abandoned
too long on the shelf go bad,
if the freshest fruits disappear

instantly, into the dark maw
of the store everyone shops for,
in blind aisles I blow a sour kiss:

*So long, friend, earth receives all
of us poor bulbs soon enough.*

The Rain Between Us

How many times your small wrists
      like the narrow ankles of deer vanish

into the underbrush! Impenetrable
      as winter rain

at airports, saying goodbye
      panic: the swift whites of your eyes
          roll out of sight,

brown animal haunches shudder
      and move away.

Under a whisper of dry leaves
      like razors

the rain between us falls
      always cold, at a distance

      that is no one's fault
         or everyone's, why feelings

wear gloves, hide themselves
      at the far edge of the forest...

              I beg you to come nearer.

Years ago, at the hospital
      when Mother was dying we embraced

just barely, shy of each other as two horses
      standing in a cold field.

Perhaps we were too close
      growing up,

perhaps I frightened you with my bright
        older sister's
                chatter.

Since then there have been long silences,
        caves in echoing woods,

but now there are steel traps
        in the far off, trembling country
                you ran away from us to live in

I'm still frightened, it's the same thing,
                the animals are still at it,

snarling over the white body
        of elegant Beirut this time

with bombs chattering, blind tanks
                you're caught all over again, don't you see

when we meet next time, in the open
        at long last let me say it

in my own voice, naked
                as the raw sounds of home,

Come back to your life and live it
        before you lose it take hold of it

with your two hands that are not hooves
        nor weapons either, but sisters
                that talk, that lift things together.

Women's Workshop

(FOR BETTE, LIZ, SALLY AND SHERYL)

Doors closed, windows. In dry August
heat, the buzz of lavender and neon
twilight coming down.

Why is there no air?

The women are talking about
poetry, of all things, they are perfect-
ly animated, almost too merry with each other but why?

*

What I want to say
is for all of us but it's not easy.

In low, cracked voices

every day more men
and women speak of their childhoods

bravely but with such delicately flaming
pink cheeks I can hardly hear them, why?

*

Core of the fruit, glowing.

Where the sugar ferments
toads fall from the women's mouths

and swear words, whenever they try to speak
openly to each other.

Squirming in their seats from the windless
humidity, the oppression,

to dig in is to dig out:

over such hard
needle and pen work
they keep laughing, they are always serious

*

But too close together: each breathes
what the other breathes

because outside it's too dangerous.

The summer sidewalks are glacial,
in freezing belches of exhaust

on every street, shameless
fat Buicks, the solid steel haunches

of nightmare fathers, grandfathers
and patriotic uncles

greedy, pointing their stiff fingers

like sinister posters that want *you*
and all your family, in icy

glittering silence glide by . . .

*

Control everywhere, and cold.
Except inside here, in the heat.

If only one of our brothers
would come inside and join us.

But still no breath
other than the women's stirs.

Against the motionless organdy of slightly
dusty white curtains

honesty tries to cover itself

but cannot: if we are to succeed
we must strip off all the bandages.

*

To know the cold is to enter it.

And then come back to the fire
with words strong enough to embrace

whatever happens, marry even the most manipulative
reasonable arguments to deep, nourishing

figures that flash and burn.

*

But flushed, twisted by too many memories,

men in the bedroom too soon
and mothers too meek to stop them,

the hostess hides herself in soft clouds
of desperate unknowing.

Plump as she is, with honey-
colored curly hair radiating,

in wise poems, warm
and innocent as milk

she studies philosophy only:

Hannah Arendt shivering
in a concentration camp, the medieval

women mystics, their pinched faces secret
as apples in a barrel

*

And the others try to agree: with smooth
hair folded around gray eyes

one of them speaks of locker rooms,
gymnasiums where she would be trapped

by pogo sticks bigger than she was, squeezed
into corners until she learned to fight back

with poems made out of toothpicks,
complicated nests for turning

anything, even the most prickly
powerful engines into toy

racing cars with gold stars stuck
under their hoods for good conduct.

*

Which makes the third woman wince:

for all her periwinkle eyes, her freckles,
under a pretty spray
of apricot hair she remembers

the bull suddenly in her path, the drill sergeant
in the sullen fire of motorcycles

roaring after her, snorting with such fury

in the cramped living room she speaks carefully,
with poems tender as tricycles but sharp, button button

she's got it, cheerfully
Southern funny, keeping one eye out

*

For the fourth woman, prim as a teacher one minute,

the next scrunched up in her seat
like shiny aluminum foil wiggling.

Around the world hitchhiker come back
in a faded dress, with black artichoke
spiked hair quivering,

her poems like hot drops
of water on a griddle jump up

like weeds in the grass, like sad mangoes
that melt in the mouth like changeable silk weaving

and shifting into bruised peaches, the faintly
pink taste of cruelty when she was too young

*

In a room much like this one, why?

The women huddle together, they drink tea
and pretend they don't know

whatever she says affects all of us:

the fourth woman's poems choke
on large, cigar-smoking

uncles like battered Chevrolets
looming over her, crushing her in a closet

*

And the uncles seem to be winning.

With swollen knuckles, with hard fingers laid
like sausages on thin knees

outside the house, on streets
up to their necks in snow

red white and blue limousines gun their motors,
the flag waves from its pole.

*

And still the women keep trying:
as I do, however tentative the lesson,

deep below words sweating
in the body's tangled jungles

as throats pound, their black
pulsing blood insists

each one of us must speak.

*

Though we know nothing as fragile
as the slender thread of metaphor's anything like strong enough

to bridge the invisible, connect
inner silence to outer
what we rely on is our figures:

carefully catwalking our way out
along poetry's tightropes, image by image extending

out of sealed rooms,
out of stifled power humming

*

In the little relief of talking about it, saying

Yes, this is what it's like
for me, how is it for you,

in the spiderwebbed orchard we keep spinning the locked, secret

isolated chambers of the body into words
in long, wavering lines laced together, stretched

from the silkworm center of lives

*

At the core of the universe, glowing.

In the steamy kitchen the women
like good witches mutter:

wedged into this burning
summer furnace

as the hitchhiker speaks of hunger
vs. fat, cigar-shaped

million-dollar bombers

a door opens, in the orange
sudden glare of rage

deep underground, pale
lips open like animals,

*

And though there are no knives here
but needling words, in the fierce

anguished intimacy of this room

there's no avoiding it: what I want to say
is for all of us and it may not work,

but still it goes on, this stern
desperate digging:

as the women stoop to it,
even as nuclear weapons carrying

trains rush by into nowhere

they keep polishing it, their vulnerable
slippery armor, link by link stitching it

into tiny shields, blazing
delicate ladders of sweat gathering,

glistening behind bent knees.

V THE POINT OF EMPTINESS

Shadow

I say to You Halt
I say to You Stop It
This is not the way to go
Your body has shriveled up
That used to loom at us like thunder
Your body is nothing but an echo
That used to shine at us like a hydrofoil
Striding over the sea
I say to You nothing is safe any more
Not even breath
I say to You we are drying up
I say to You we have raisins for souls
Even when I drop mine into water
It won't swell, I say to You *No wings, No wings*
And You made us
Not even humor seems to be able to elevate us,
What is that strange stink in the air
Is it gas? Is it radioactive? Is it safe?
No wonder people think I'm crazy
Up here on the rooftops waving my megaphone
Stop shouting, they tell me
Go back to your knitting, milk your own veins
And forget about ours, we have our own rows to ruin

But the stairs I'm standing on are folding
And theirs too,
You better listen to me, Shadow
What goes up must come down
This morning I woke up muttering
Speak to me in lilies but I'm not a lily
I'm sick, I'm a dead prune
Why did You dress us in petals
In the first place, turning on our stems
Like numb barber poles blubbering
He loves me, He loves me not
When I go under for the last time, when the air

Slides out of me like a fishing line or a trombone
That won't stop,
What have You given me to hold onto,
You said it was our fault
And it is but then You left us
Why did You close Your mouth at us
In the name of all the little dried apricots
And babies, especially the babies
When the great blast of holocaust cracks the sky
And the book of the world wide open
I say to You Halt
I say to You Stop It
This is no way to go
I'm talking to You, Shadow

Whatever Gray Grid

bristling, as in a thicket
                    of black raspberries
     the thoughts i think i think
clutch at each other, sticky
                tiny hard seeds
     creaking minute axles
              stuck in there,
                  the pits of them

however furiously we keep hacking
                  at the stiff chain gang
       of the sentence
     pigeons swoop,
              clouds over the city
              or bears
              in distant parks waddle

numbed in their brown studies
                  brilliant psychopaths
   and scientists
              keep struggling after them,
                digit by digit hooked
from one node to another
              in blurred brambles flashing
   over an invisible network
              of delicate red rope

green paper spins
              speedily into the wastebasket
  in the steel prickles of the printout
              whatever gray grid
        may focus

the doe behind the bushes
                         never appears:
                    touch it
                and the cell divides,
            under a microscope
                         the bird vanishes
            as soon as it's out of the mouth

Some Nights the Mind

What is the shape of shapelessness

In the echoing vaults the mind knows
Not to speak of it but to fall into it

From its own precarious cliffs skirting the universe
In the dead twist of walls coming together

Some nights the mind sees itself plummeting

Silent as Icarus, a wrecked plane disappearing
Into the forehead of Atlantis, yet another soul

Dropped out of heaven, from proud daylight
Into inner dark

Hundreds of fish faces peer in, lazy as angels
Drifting by

What we are looking for here is the one face
That will not fade

In a welter of other memories, the flood
Of a mind awash in itself

The events of the day, what happened exactly
In all its dazzling detail

May never be known

Because there are waters beyond the waters
Of the brain

We cannot stop ourselves from being invaded

By whatever lies out there:
Depth charges, doomed cities

Spilled onto the ocean floor

The crowned heads we loved, their profiles
Pressed into crusted gold and then scattered

In the jumble of last things,

In the movie the crowded suitcase
Full of waterlogged loot splits open

Because it was too heavy to carry

Because we do not believe there are waters
Beyond the waters

What remains is a faint tingling sensation,

A tooth slowly crumbling away
Into its own cavities

Like a snail looking for its other foot

On the roof of the mouth the tongue
Lumbers through its red currents

Like thick seaweed cut off at the roots

The Point of Emptiness

But the point of emptiness is that it's always there
Even though we can't see it, it keeps out of sight
In all that matters, insubstantial as air.

You keep looking for it, in your mid-fifties you swear
You'll thread the needle somehow, knowing it must be right
The point of emptiness is that it's always there,

And even though it's important for camels to strip bare
Of extra baggage, in readiness for transworld flight
Into all that matters, insubstantial as air,

Finally it makes no difference: standing on the massive stair
And straining upwards, into the vast hole of midnight
The point of emptiness is that it's always there

If only we could believe in it, and then not have to care
That the pupil's tiny opening is our only insight
Into all that matters, insubstantial as air

And yet not: as $E = MC^2$,
As the weight of the whole world spins into the light,
The point of emptiness is that it's always there
In all that matters, insubstantial as air.

Near Zero

small window in the tight
wall around us

opens

at night, at the edge of a dim ocean
"we don't know the half of"

wooden shell like an ear

strains after the slow
liquid drop of the town clock's

ringing

each wet plate of it
spreads out like oil

over the rooftops disappearing

like a lone rowboat
or a sea gull

out there riding the black swells
we should be riding

ourselves

as rings circle the earth
slowly, counting the passing

hours

here in the flickering silence

one hand like a fist
that belongs to no one

drops back to the ground

in the sea's boundless throat
mirror with no stars in it

harmonics multiply and divide
and divide again

near zero

but nothing ever flares
of its own accord, defiant

wing across the sky

back at the window
again

the bell keeps ringing midnight

and then one
and one and one

again

the next birth cry
and the next

leaps out, clangourous
and then quiet

and quieter still, in ripples

carried beyond ourselves
to the rim of the world and back

finally it's so faint
impossible to predict

fraction upon fraction

across the water tongues
thin wires stretch

so far who can hear them
not even the animals

no one

VI THE COLOR OF HISTORY

The Color of History

The rug silent, a snowfield. Bordered in light brown
orange Mexican squares. Where the green tweed
leafy sofa sits with its arms open, windows splash light
down from the bald mountains, spilling over the mute
untraceable oak floor like melted butter.

                              Tides sweep through this room: in the afternoon
small, off-campus classes, students
brushing the mud off, drumming their rubber sneakers
nervously, waiting for the teacher
who sweeps in and out with them, one moment
flourishing pen and paper, weekends in and out of the kitchen

                              as friends, men and women, gather
at the cherrywood table, sputtering over their wine
and roast lamb, even as the roar of far off battles
foams over dinner plates and recedes,
occasional ideas put in an appearance, dazzling

                              lighthouses flash out over the waves
and everyone rushes up to agree
or disagree, passions red as radishes erupt over clenched fists
and pinched eyebrows, then subside into loose
hands waving goodbye, see you next time,

                              but the very next day, or soon after,
another friend, desperate, weeps on the secondhand
fuchsia armchair, digging her nails into it because she can't stand it,
what have the most recent, even the most dangerous
strategic missiles got to do with *her*,

                              why should she care
about the latest revolution in El Salvador, even the trees
dying everywhere, she can't help it, life's got her
like a worm in a bird's beak, shaking her so hard

finally even the tall fig tree on the end table
pays attention, the husband and the wife listen

                                   and then she's gone, the room collects itself
for the next round, while the couple eat a late supper
in the kitchen, explaining her to each other
as well as they can, in the living room the coffee table,
the polished rocks in their bowls, the driftwood in its twisted shapes,
the books in their bindings wait patiently until later,

                                        as the pair quietly reads
on the green sofa, pages rustling, once in awhile soft
combers on a beach, brief surges to the threshold
of whose consciousness, the curtains hold their breath
and so do the pictures on the walls,

                                     each individually
handcrafted gay square keeps watch; carefully rendered snails,
lopsided dogs, small stick figures go about their business
but keep peering, against oblivion they stare out
over the couple's heads at the sky
beyond the plate glass windows. On a clumsily framed piece
of shaggy barkcloth, for instance,

                                 two shorter than usual, partially skewed
Tarascan sweethearts lead each other up a hill
that figures in no history book ever: helping each other along
they tiptoe between yellow pigs
and purple butterflies, birds like raised eyebrows flying

                                awkwardly, almost out of the picture
and into the next one, the bright oilcloth heaven of a Syrian
slightly off kilter horse on a baby blue background prancing
with fierce nostrils flaring, spurred on by the heels
of a black, gorgeously dressed knight surrounded by kindergarten
monkeys, raggedy lions, pink popcorn flowers

                         right next to the coffee and chocolate colored
Hmong story cloth with its neatly stitched villagers
leaving their homes forever, trekking past orange tigers, peculiar
white squirts of bombs, helicopters, from there onto overcrowded
boats under bigger than people sea gulls heading for America
with its shiny colleges, its couples who collect folk art

                              to keep themselves company, why not,
against the great silences of night, especially when they're upstairs
asleep now, all personality erased, over the clear shapes
of the Black Prince, the Hmong villagers, even the determined
Tarascan couple climbing, opposite the one painting

                              with no one in it, a bleak
December landscape where almost everything's disappeared
finally into the ground, its slate blue shadows stretched
over the snowfield in the center, the whole tapestry
of busy weeds, of frozen grasses vanished

                              into empty squadrons of light looming
over all but a few featureless clumps
of low willows hunched, clotted along the river bottom
like old blood, across the canvas the scabbed
dark red, somber maroon bushes
the color of history, the husband once said.

VII THE LAKE ITSELF

The Story

Begins the moment we wake up, it's the way we tell each other
We want our lives to be, in the *Daily Chronicle*, over coffee
And glazed doughnuts, sometimes even standing in the check-out line
What he did and then what she did, whatever happened
Is dry bones, is withered acorn until we water it with words,
Until we tell it to walk, nobody knows how
Anything happens until we say it, today, for instance
The story is that I got up, scrubbed the sleep from my eyes
And loved you all day long because who would I be
Without you, even the smartest, least narcissistically self-
Conscious tree in a forest or a poem can't realize itself
Let alone fall, with nobody there to care about it: the story may not

Even be all that interesting, but thank goodness anyway,
When Janet stopped by the house, hungry
And still running on European time, there was cold borscht in the
    refrigerator
And cold tongue, left over, with horseradish and raisin sauce,
And even though the stories she told about Yugoslavia
And traveling there with her sick mother swarmed
Around the kitchen like black flies over a corpse
Stiff as the forsythia bush in the backyard
That's dead all right, winterkilled, I checked it out myself:
So, no fountains of it, no great sprays of yellow rain
Will be falling for us this season, nevertheless we still laughed
And went on gossiping, eating the cold soup,

Though the story at the afternoon conference was by some Frenchman
Who thinks America's made up, a fantasist's dream of a Disneyland
With no people in it, only the flickering *hyperreality* of TV
Commercials invisibly running the entire cartoon country,
A story of course many of my colleagues at school
Believe in, they listened to the French savant
Politely, nodding and smiling as even the two babies in jumpsuits
Crawling on the floor among us muted their cries,
But others refused to go along with it: Bill reminded us

That the traditional European view of the noble, now ignoble
But still charmingly romantic savage never met a real
Deerfly infested forest or an Oklahoma dust storm in its life,

While Howard, hunched in on himself like a black bear
Spoke into the heavy slab of his beard grumbling
About all the rest of us, people like you and me getting up,
Having lunch with each other or shopping or harvesting corn
Or wheat or potatoes, in the vast, unwritten-about stretches of land
Between New York and Los Angeles tending our own gardens
And minding our business, as like and as unlike
Even the funniest French philosophers as possible,
But really the story is that nothing, as usual, was decided. Beside me
Bette listened attentively, beneath the luminous cloud
Of her fair hair, her face like a drowsy Madonna
Serious under the track lights, the cries of the scholars and the babies

Until we went on to the next chapter, to Botany Hall
To listen to a student's thesis reading: Michael,
Ex-naval officer ex-logger ex-teacher turned poet
And also ambulance driver reading us poems
About what *he* fights for, in classrooms and on the road
The lives of schoolchildren and grownups sputtering out
On streets in front of bars, only a few minutes
At the end of each day to think about the story
Of living here, right here in America, with people who used to think
We shouldn't make war on anyone, how is it possible
The story winds down so fast, but it picks up
Almost immediately, right after supper you went off

To play poker with your friends the history professor
And the would-be writer from Reno and the *Old World Honey* beekeeper
And distributor who does research on condors
In Peru, in between studying piano and trout fishing;
While I finished the dishes to the music
Of a terrible but strangely interesting performance of the Archduke
On Public Radio, by friends of mine in town,
Music students, actually, but when Janet called to commiserate we agreed

That live amateur is better than dead professional
Anytime, but then the story is that I turned on the television
And suddenly the whole day turned into John Gielgud
In a concentration camp, with heaped bodies piled up

Like stacked lumber, miserable yellow cadavers rolling
Right into the living room, between the real news camera footage
And the kodachrome fiction I was struck dumb, speechless,
I wept inwardly and groaned, all my limbs trembled
About to be cut down, my tongue turned to a stump
At the mercy of every ax, as if this were actually the Old Testament
Mindlessly veering, in a world so full of malice
And blind prophets, the story is that we live
However we can, in thick forests rustling our leaves,
Like tall trees listening carefully to each other
And holding each other up, how can it possibly matter what's real
And what's not.

The Dance Hall

For what if they're all there already,
What if the sweet soupy music of the dance band's already insinuating itself
Under their spry feet,

What if your plump mother's still whirling around in the old waltz
With you safe in her arms,

What if your older brother's still flashing his bold tricky smile
Over the polished floor, what if your favorite uncle never went bankrupt
In Florida, with the last of your father's big bucks,

What if your tall serious sister stayed home, never got drunk
On Pink Ladies, never cried herself to sleep,

What if your Irish grandmother never groaned, sighed
Or crossed herself, or clicked her yellow teeth?

Each evening you imagine them
Deliberately, the way they cannot be

Ever again, nowadays we know bodies dissipate themselves
Into rarer and rarer arrangements,

But what if the 50th wedding anniversary couple with their hearing aids
Really did live forever,

What if the smallest Girl Scout, the one with the crooked spectacles
Is still selling cookies, UNICEF cards for the poor,

What if the guy next to you on the night shift is still coughing
And smoking, his Buick never got trashed,

Your friend who went off to war came right back
With all his legs intact, no wheelchair

Ever entered his life, he's a famous mountain climber now
With four children, the dance hall's on his ranch

And the tough little kid next door, the one with the pogo stick
Did not die on the operating table, somewhere he's still clapping his hands

And hopping around to the music, so what if it's all nothing
But wishes? Dry wisps of paper

In the rickety prayer wheel of the brain flutter
Like used film clips to be thrown away

Or held onto, projected one more time,
What other life is there
But these long ago partners flashing across the sky,

While you stand in the shadows with Jane Austen, Tommy Dorsey,
Tennessee Williams, even Shakespeare, why not?

This way you can have them all back
Whenever you want to,

It's summer, the music croons to them,
Swooping and dipping and twirling

With wild roses, clumps of mosquitoes idling
Over fat rowboats tied up at the June boat docks,

Maybe they could go on like this forever, in the old waltzes
They keep looking over their shoulders and smiling, waiting for you.

Letter to Jonathan from Missoula

Well sure yes, nowadays maybe a lot of poems do look like doodles
scrawled on a paper doily at the world's grubbiest
fast food joint. Stained with maroon ketchup
and cigarette burns, it's the fossilized remains
of hard thought, playing cards, matches, etc.
that stick longest: maybe they do only emerge out of
"the inner world of mere feelings", but in this century between inner

and outer we know there's no easy
distinction possible; still, whether the spots on the tablecloth,
the excavated clay bowls in a tomb
or the blips on a radar screen are food
for real or imaginary journeys and how sweet
or sour they'll be, *that's* what we need to know,

even at Pompeii we wish there had been more graffiti,
in photographs even the widest of open mouths
out of context is only an ominous howling or a shout
in a silent film unless there are words for it,
whether it's "merely" obsessed poetry "reacting"
with petrified jaws to a sky suddenly choked
with smothering ash, no wonder the exhausted doodler
can't stop: as year after year keeps
spewing forth new leaves, this morning
for instance, strolling to work through spring's
rococo petit point, its lime green leafy lace

ahead of me on the path suddenly I saw a strange cameo of a man
dapper, in a black, exquisitely cut silk suit
that showed off his waist, his thin shoulders, the neat patent leather
crisp cubes of his feet but above all, astonishingly
in our aggressively casual community of hairy
but earnest students, he'd topped himself off with a hat,
a Fedora actually, under the sophisticated snap of its brim
sleek as a pair of scissors tap tapping along
as if he were under glass, in the great shaggy Northwest

he seemed incredibly *finished*, even sinister
but only for a moment: the next thing that popped up
at the gates of the campus was a comfortable loud group

of two scruffy youths on bicycles, each dragging
a dog behind on a leash, bright polka dot bandannas
hanging around all four necks like loose diapers
and a puppy waddling after. One boy was saying
something about "the random activities of DNA
cells in the latest nuclear generator", if we could only
get right in there with them, stop time,
enter it for a second, but only to go with it,
see what it feels like, when a young mother

in flowered purple and yellow shorts, also on a bicycle
almost bumped into them, hauling behind *her*
a go-cart with a red-faced baby in it, sporting
in his case not exactly a hat but a tough looking
child-sized helmet on his blond head, over which
the two older boys almost fell off their bicycles with friendliness,
"*Hi!*" shouting at the young woman, "How *are* you?"

as the stiff figure of the stranger neatly sidestepped
the group's ragged circle, mincing along
like a black ant across a tablecloth, carefully
skirting all obstacles, under the giant scrutiny
of the school clock tower stuck always just past the hour
until he was far down the path, mysteriously tiny
as a steel hairpin dwindling into its own perspectives

while I, helpless to keep up with him, of course fell
flat on my face before the sheer razzle-dazzle of it all,
in a flounder of feelings stunned, struck dumb in my tracks
by the bicycle group's radiant, gloriously goofy faces blazing
against the gray sidewalk like some mindlessly 20th century
American icon of the wild, untamably vanishing
live territory all of us must leave behind.

Directions To Go On With

Or just let it go, let it drift
from doorstep to doorstep, scattered

semi-transparent dust.

One tiny thrust
and the astronaut leaps

to the ceiling after his
spaghetti

delicate veins dangle
like threads from an old sweater

sometimes cottonwood fluff

blows itself into small heaps
in corners

these occasionally shape themselves
into words, fuzzy

directions to go on with

Love   Poem   Idea
we like to tell ourselves we think

sweet woodsmelling chips fly
from the spine's puzzled   trunk

scuttle across fields

scraps of breath   feathers
on green   airy pool tables

sentenced into order

across the lawn dandelions
gray puffballs   body

English themselves from one
vague pocket to another

each morning the lint
of dreams sidles across the forehead

each evening sparks
of fire float   to the sky

thought breaks away
out of its handcuffs   Houdini

dies and is born again
over and over, helpless

rockets rise   unstoppable

endless, among the nebulae
burning motes of light

ice crystal among ice crystals

trackless swan   invisible
white seed slipping

Spaceship Voyager on its journey

soars outwards whispering
Love   Poem   Idea

Deer Crossing, Wild Horse Island

(FOR NANCY, HENRY, SARAH, AND EMILY HARRINGTON)

Privileged, this one day off
          on winter ski slopes hushed,
              high above town skidding
      to a sudden, icy stop,
            across the trail we see them,
        deer like dark boxes jerk
                among the trees quick
             coiled springs up to their hips
    in deep powder but still moving

So fast how can anyone be certain
        whatever we say or see may
           or may not be true,
       down here at my dogged
          timid deliberations, who am I
            to say anything,
    among all these thrusting
        young trees what is there to do?
  Though smothered trunks call out
            for help like muffled
       tongues under heavy snowpack

Eventually it will melt
       of its own accord,
        even in the high pastures
      of Montana, where there are few newspapers,
        only one or two ruined
      cellar holes, low fences left behind,
    on Wild Horse Island deer walk
            gravely, calm princes
        and princesses, in and out
          of thick groves,
      in willow and juniper the kingdom
        is theirs and they know it,

Even in cities they peer out
                    from every corner, from amplified
         expensive blasters, black
                         silvery boxes for fast-
talking giraffes, for curly-haired young girl
              elands jazzing around in
         red miniskirts, even among motorcycles
         and crack advertising executives

Like fizz from the finest soda water;
                    sooner or later its sparkles
                         drearily sputter and bog down
              into gray gutters, the rigid
                              smothering safety of routine
              that never changes, but Stop!

Though no one can ever be present
                    more than a moment to capture
         anything, least of all
                    on paper, truth's what
         we never stop looking for,
                         once we have seen it, plunging
    through deep snow or even
                    in slatted, broken-bottled
         back alleys, Slow

Children Crossing, or Deer
                    along the highway it's the sign
              not the certainty saves us,
         keeps us in air, alert
                    on steep slopes moving
                              with blurred shapes hiding
              all around us, lazily
                         startling up from the heart
              on Wild Horse Island leaping
         across fences, across walls.

Frontier

In the middle of Kansas some kid's still hot-rodding around
In a secondhand sports car, streetlights pooling on his face
Like neon strobes in a dance hall. At the stops he throttles down,
Then revs up, maniacal as any cowboy
Out there gunning down lone Main Street at midnight
With a Jack Nicholson grin for starters: could he maybe play the piano
Like Nicholson did, on a truck in a traffic jam
Or what? What can he do?
Join the Air Force? Finish Graduate School?

He's really worried about it, you can tell by the way he laughs.
His hair flips forward and he keeps brushing it back,
Past Colonel Sanders Chicken and the used car lots grazing,
Saddled into his red leather bucket seat
Suddenly he can't stand it! He tromps down hard
And then pours it on: how fast can he go?
At the city limits, where the houses begin to thin out,
The black spaces between towns expand
Directionless as the ocean but empty, empty as the sky
Between one cluster of lights and the next
Is there no movement but his? He sees the red wink
Of a plane spurt across the night, he imagines people
Talking to each other inside, cups clinking, stewardesses in the aisles

But then he turns on his Mozart: Live! Action! Music!
In the car's closed capsule, from the expensive tape deck pouring
The pure silvery beads bubble and pop
Like rain after a long drought, like rapids in a river
Almost they pull him under but the flute soars upward,
The ecstatic mathematics of the symphony fill the air
With cathedrals of such absolute clarity he stands up in the stirrups
Like a madman on the 4th of July, he bangs the wheel for joy!

Behind the windshield he's trembling, panting with terrified love
Because somewhere his girl's waiting for him, she wants them to get married

And so do his folks, but back there in town he'd be lost:
If Country Western's what they want, sure, he can complain
With the best of them, how will he ever,
Ever stand his own loneliness? His sweetheart's snuggled in
With cashmere arms and an apron, in the little house next door
Soup's on, the warmth of it steams his glasses

Till he can't see for a second but then he turns up the volume,
Sluicing himself in the glass waterfall of the music,
The alto horns cooing, the high peaks of the violins like mountains
Graphed by hundreds of wildflowers, tingling carpets of notes
In such exquisite mysteries of precision shimmering
He thinks he can ride right through them and on out
To the farthest boundaries of the known world

If only he weren't so suspicious of himself!
He thinks maybe he only likes Mozart
Because *Amadeus* was such a great movie; besides
What is all this running around?
Like the movie said, genius makes its own rules
But what if he's kidding himself?
Out there in the black crystal of night,
The sheer dizziness of his delight in it,
Roaring along in the car singing and shouting, is this just an excuse

Or what? At parties he keeps asking his friends for advice
But what do they know? The cattle in the fields he passes
Look up solemnly, now that the West is won
You'd think these kids would settle down now wouldn't you,
But he just pulls at the snap brim
Of his Humphrey Bogart felt hat
And pokes the speedometer up into the red
Danger territory:
Long past midnight he's still out there on the strip
Lassoing himself around in big circles, heart galloping,
Boot stomping, the pulse in his temples pounding,
In the prairies inside his head he keeps seeing numbers,

Green flickering digits that turn into far off satellites,
As they photograph Saturn at last he keeps thinking about whalesong
Nobody ever heard of until it was recorded and brought home

And then released into space;
As the small dots of the music ride out
Across the fields of heaven, the distant spheres revolving
Out there beyond the last gas station wheeling
Like geese in their high echelons, invisible harmonies plunge
Like wild surging horses, over the dark charts of the stars
Huge delicate herds of them still sweep through some crazy kid's car.

Each Day the Mind Rises

At the end of Ireland, Gallaurus
                    the eighth century empty
            solitary cell stares out
    at the Western Sea, where the singular
                        strange monk who huddled there
        in his stone hut built to last
    kept satellite watch out
            endlessly on the heavens,
                how they revolve

                        *

And nowadays, even as the adolescent
                    skateboard expert with his body
            chops, macadam jolts
                    gives every adult
            the finger,
        though the mother-to-be cries out
            "I'm too young!" the weight
        of the future pressing on her, she gives up
        her precarious privacy gladly
                    in the cell of herself tipping

                        *

As each day the mind rises
                out of its own belittlement –
        how many pills, which pair
                    of socks to put on –
    though the paper says 10° below and the electric
                    furnace says stay home, the father
                        picks up his heavy
            stiff briefcase,
            struggles out into the cold
    as much a part of it as anyone, even

*

Those gray outcasts dreaming
        in front of blackboards, with oddly matched
            cheap shoes but with pencils
     like knives, among the stars faster
        than computers,
              scribbling new paths
    they keep guzzling it, the lonely
         excitement at the edge,
            the heady froth rising
     in the wild windsurfer leaning
far out, lashed to the mast of himself, over
          the blown peaks of the sea

*

So the 747 walks the tightrope
         between Washington and Paris
    with the Emperor Concerto like a palace
           parading through our earphones
    with Pop, or Rock, or Folk Music
         separate, whichever we choose
    with the brash sun coming up
          out one window, the moon
    veiling itself in the other,
  in the cockpit, at the very tip
         of the whole journey the watchful
    grownup kid at the controls
         churns his feet to propel our paddle-wheel
  boat through the sky

*

As sailors watch it, from below
         vaulting as high as possible, the drone
    of an imprisoned bee throbbing
         against the stained glass

ceiling of the turning world
        even the passengers feel it, their foreheads
                    pressed against dark plastic
up there among blinking
        low red and green lights
with trembling legs locked
                forever in the lone, teetering
    brief chair of each man
                    and each woman's narrow
peculiar path through the air

The Wind that Swept Up Great Homer

*"What are the chances you just inhaled a molecule which Caesar
exhaled in his dying breath? The surprising answer is that, with
probability greater than 99%, you did just inhale such a
molecule."* — John Allen Paulos, Innumeracy

Lazing around in the body like the loose strings
            of yawns, shrugs, suddenly rustling leaves, taps on the
                        inner windows,
        air doesn't have to send messages:
            its agents have already infiltrated
    everywhere, inside the lungs sliding
                    from cell to cell,
                at each new pressure shifting
        daily, in the slow heave
                of ocean against invisible
                    red walls
    faceless as the smell of blood
                on the kitchen table, intimate
                as the odor of one's own breath
                    it swirls through the body's streets
        or folds itself like an eagle
                high up in the attic;
                        in the temple of the winged pelvis
            if it has soft hands
        also it has teeth for gnashing,
    it inhabits its own hollows with darkness, don't deny it
            but ride with it, ride with it
    dissolving ahead of us like music
                in "despised poems"; in the caught breath
            at 2 A.M. on the phone as the strange voice
    tells about the accident, the
                death while we were sleeping,
        always, especially when we're not there,
    it keeps moving, restless
                as it is calm
            and then not calm,

turning and turning on itself in clouds
boiling across the planet,
the shape of it is a gesture
we recognize from within, high in the mountains
as snow hurls itself into flags, brilliant
banners streaming away,
telescopes reach out, craning
beyond the wildest weather,
even in outer space
the moon lifts itself into seas
we know because we named them,
stunned by the silver glitter
of poplar leaves turning over
or combers on the beach, their motions
are the same everywhere;
beauty lives in the body
or never, its breathing roams the hallways
at the office, on the front porch
the long whistling sough of it
lifts the hair on the neck
like antelope fur, lonely
in the vast sea of the world as whales,
it forgives everything because it moves everything,
even in Times Square wheezing
through millions of mouths,
down every blind alleyway
the wind that swept up great Homer
still swells in the belly,
in every billowing sail
and slack lungful pouring
out over the plains
and back in again, cramped,
rising and falling, still
it will not be contained
even when it is shut up
right here in the living room,
at the movies, in bed at night
homely as a child's quick

                              animal cry
           often you can hear it
                              in the farthest field like a horse
silky with rain, its chestnut sides heaving
                          out over the pasture this one, mysteriously
              profound sigh

The Lake Itself

"Becoming conscious is of course a sacrilege
against nature, it is as though you had
robbed the unconscious of something."
                    – Jung, "Zarathustra"

As we come up out of it each morning

Shaking our heads to scatter the last bright drops
Of clarity that still cling to us

We can't believe it,
It seems so much like sleep, and sleep so much like water

We feel it in our fingers all day long.

And though it is perfectly ordinary, its chill
Sparkling presence calm

As it is eloquent, it keeps tempting us to return,
Heave our homesick selves

Through pale lozenges of light to the profound
Shadowy purple and deep middle beyond.

For all day, breathing

Heads up, far from the delicious wet
We can't help remembering:

As stones at the bottom touch motionless toes,
Rub shoulders with no fish near the edges

But glow quietly in their whiteness
Like teeth in a glass of tap water, their buried reds

And mottled blues glimmer back up at us

As strange as they are familiar, their soft radiance
Doomed, dangerous, flickering there in the half light

Like a dead empress' jewels heaped
On the floor of a giant tomb.

But now we are finally awake
And dried off, sitting here on the bank

In Western deserts where are we?

In the grit of the daily routine,
In the gray, peppery choke

Of smoke everywhere, in the forest fires of our lives

Sometimes we open our eyes
Only to be scoured away

By charred ash, in swirls of blowing sand

The beloved feast crumbles
As soon as we clutch at it, with fists

That hold neither dust nor water.

And yet it is still there, the lake

That great flattened out whale
Of a shining body stretched

On the left hand, below the huckleberry bushes
Its shimmering grid reminds us

In the slow, thirsty suck
Of small mouths, waves lapping at the body's

Frilled edges, suppose we are sunken rowboats
In someone else's dream? With strange voices

And sighs, with sea gulls passing over
The lake itself,

Even on dry land it is there

Deep underground, its currents live in us
As we in them, in swaying hammocks of sleep

Fish hover, fins scuffle along the bottom

In the muffled rhythms of the rich
Heavy liquids that first floated us

In endless intimacy, the ecstatic
Weightlessness of water:

As drowned jewels leap up

Again and again like dragonflies,
In quick flashes of glitter

The body never forgets a baptism,

Its first eye opening plunge into
And then out of the light.

The Periscope of the Eye

At cocktail parties submerged
But still struggling, craning my neck up
On the street talking to others
Or not talking, how keep the periscope of the eye open
Wide enough?

As the underwater days rush by
Fists knock at my hull, political prisoners
And South African refugees reach for me in the dark,

But with all my bells going off, electrically wired gates,
Like everyone else there are groceries I must buy, taxes,
My family's heads to be held up
Right now, of course there's never enough time

To think about how trapped we are, how terrified
Of drowning, of losing ourselves in the ocean
Out there with all those others...

My friend says to be able to bear it
We must put on our blinders at the train station,
But once everyone's aboard, in the subway's oddly marine light
There's no calm, no float
And no salt, either.

In the backwaters of earth, in poverty, in oppression,
Surely people speak to each other, because there is nothing else
They sing whenever they can, sometimes they even manage
To tell each other the truth,

But here we are free to lie,
From Maine to California to Kansas
Here almost all we have are lies
We believe are true because they soothe us:

My friend says Poetry blooms best

On bread and water, even slipped through the barred
Metal hatchways of prisons,

But here Poetry is invisible:
As strange silos thrust themselves up
Out of the troughs of the unconscious
What, would you have us look out the window of opportunity
For someone else?

Pretending I don't care, hurling myself into the statistics
In the land of instant gratification I am not gratified:
The minute after I eat ice cream, O I am shriveled up,
My fat tongue drums uselessly in my mouth,

For the well fed periscope is a vacuum cleaner
Swallowing whole continents of information and then choking
On its own loneliness, who is that calling from the top deck?

Long ago it was Emerson, then Whitman with his wooden rafts,
Then Dickinson keeping the log, meticulously
Up there in the crow's nest scouting for God,

But down here what we have are a few exiles,
Granite lighthouses brandishing the great Book
And what can we do really?
On the horizon there used to be Pasternak,
Ahkmatova, Neruda trumpeting like a bull elephant

But now all we have is our own life jackets,
In steamy saunas of self help
The spirit expends itself by counting:

One drop for me, one drop for you,
And one for the itemized convoys, the trucks
That probably won't get through.

Cruising along in the one body
That keeps me and my family safe,

Now all that interests me are a few seamounts rising
Silently, from their trenches,

As one or two livid faces, hands
Waving for help flash by
And disappear instantly, on the deck
Just below the conning tower I hear footsteps,

My neighbor's stooped silhouette
And then something that looks like a child, my child!
About to be swept into the sea

Unless I can stop it, how can I,
Mouth filled with self pity,
Or any of the rest of us, drifting
To the rhythms of unknown laws

And refusing to think about it, outside
Every circle there are others
Widening and widening, already the first odd

Irritable scratches are sputtering
Over the submarine's sides like the probe
And crackle of giant claws:

As more and more power leaks from my eyes
In the blare of patriotism, myself
The sole measure, how can I say what fish
Are too big for our nets,

What immense songs may be moving
Right now, out there beyond all instruments?

Paul Bunyan's Bearskin

These days the whole hide of it lolls across the globe
            like a Paul Bunyan bearskin: numb head pointing West,
        truncated stubs of the hind legs stretched out
                over Florida and then Maine
                    as hard to hold in the mind as the definitive outline,
    bulk, depths, blurred shape of the life
            of its least citizen;

clouds of industrial speculation
                like flies over a dead body rise, pollute the entire horizon
        from North Carolina to Oregon, even as we soar above it
            in the rickety grasshopper of the self leaping
                through mists of decay, fog clinging to the eyes
    from one landing place to the next,
            the airport in Washington first, O breath-stopper,
                    Jefferson's low monument rising
                like beauty's breast, the Amazonian army of white buildings
        all hovering a few airy inches above the ground,

but next comes Harrisburg,
                this trip the dirigible almost founders
        on three sinister smokestacks, squat radioactive cans
            stuck right up out of the river;
                        as the carcass continues to fester
    in the terminal there are souvenirs, the last word in T-shirts

except if we drive beyond it,
                along the gentle Susquehanna
            in curved watery mudflats crocuses and the quiet Amish
        stand up beside small houses and lopsided billboards begging
                EAT HERE BEFORE WE BOTH GO HUNGRY

and so we do, out of this nettle pluck eggs, pluck daffodils
                and shoofly pie, berries the Indians might have eaten
        once, long ago, before the Sunday afternoon hunters
    from Chicago next, the toothed skyline wavering in the lake

where glass fronts glitter, rivers reverse themselves
in the hands of men who believe they were given claws
to pull down Ursa Major and drink from it and then sling it back up
to swing on it, from here to the farthest rings of Saturn

and back again, this time to the comfortable wooden steps
and modern riversprawl of St. Louis,
here at the broad belt line
where the eye of the arch is bigger but more humanly graceful,
where the hole in the clouds looks
upwards to the clearing heavens

and the grasshopper jumps Westward,
the mind plays leapfrog
over the toiling wagons, man and woman sized wishes
to forget murder, the black man fallen in the street,
the red flowers of rats in tenements, grizzled strip mines
and the gaunt children of the East,

so the direction is North now,
looking for the next opening,
in swirling blankets of white bees
we almost get lost, but settle down heavily through snowfields,
sheet after icy sheet of them
in Minneapolis surrounded

but stalwart still,
with fires roaring in the hearts of trappers
and bankers alike, but most in the doughty wills of voters
blunt knuckled and fingered and muscled
at the chill headwaters of the Mississippi

and then onward, out across the brown rolling ribs,
the waving emptiness of prairies to the ridged shoulders
of the next jumping off place, the dazzling white bone
of Salt Lake City reaching up
out of crowned mountains to catch wanderers and keep them

except that it can't do it,
                 the fantastic palaces of sainthood are too rich
          for the thin blood of hope,
             the one goad that keeps us going;
                      peering through the magnifying glass

at each new area on the map,
             each detailed piece of anatomy
     in startling clarity raised up to us who are still floating
              vaguely between all of them,
                  in the long milky veil of distance,
          in the smoky fur of a twilight
              that obscures all but the most ruthless, fierce clamorous rips

so full of themselves it is no wonder we veer slightly South
          to the outermost edge of it,
              the ragged beachhead of the skin
     of San Francisco, the blue pools of her bays
                  and shaggy redwoods, in deep orange over the hilltops
              the bronze wheel of a choked sun going down
          as the whole East sails in through the Golden Gate

and meets itself coming back; the corkscrew of a Piper Cub
     bumbles up the peninsula, in the dark iris of dusk
  each North South East West airport exists only to be left
          or returned to, from another:
              to try to map any one single direction

is to die into dead leather,
             the corpse pinned to coordinates no one alive can find
   twice in the same place,
              so soon geography breaks up
          into individual cities and countries,
       one-of-a-kind cells breathing
the live rippling spirit of a bear taking up his bed
          and walking, no one can predict how or when or where.

Patricia Goedicke is the author of nine collections of poetry, the most recent of which, *The Tongues We Speak* (Milkweed Editions, 1989), was a 1990 *New York Times Book Review* Notable Book of the Year. Her poetry has received several national grants and awards, including a National Endowment for the Arts Fellowship. She has recently received the University of Montana's Distinguished Scholar Award for creative activity.

Educated at Middlebury College and Ohio University, Ms. Goedicke has taught poetry at Hunter College, Sarah Lawrence College, Ohio University, and the Instituto Allende of the University of Guanajuato in San Miguel de Allende, Mexico. Currently she teaches in the University of Montana's Creative Writing Program in Missoula, Montana, where she lives with her husband, Leonard Wallace Robinson.

*Typeset in Pilgrim
by The Typeworks.
Printed on acid-free Glatfelter
by Edwards Brothers.
Designed by Norman Fritzberg
with the assistance of R. W. Scholes.*

POETRY
$11.00

PAUL BUNYAN'S BEARSKIN
Poems by Patricia Goedicke

Paul Bunyan's Bearskin is a generous, dazzling collection about the life of mind and body in a fragmented body politic. Patricia Goedicke's previous book of poems, *The Tongues We Speak* (Milkweed Editions), was a New York Times Book Review Notable Book for 1990.

Praise for Patricia Goedicke's poetry:

"Goedicke has trained her eyes and ears and heart on the faltering culture of late twentieth-century America, and her vision helps us clarify our own." —*The Hungry Mind Review*

"Although not narrowly political, her work shows an attentiveness to the world and where we are in history . . . nearly always one is struck by the strength of her emotion, her sincerity, a memorable rhythm and her attention to the world . . ." —*The New York Times Book Review*

"Goedicke has been compared to Whitman in her use of the extended line, and because she seeks to bring the entire world into the poem . . . The profound feel for rhythm, swing, and modulation of the human voice is astonishing and makes Goedicke's poetry a great physical pleasure to read." —*New Letters*

ISBN 0-915943-54-9

MILKWEED EDITIONS